Birds and Beasts

BIRDS AND BEASTS

William Jay Smith

Woodcuts by
Jacques Hnizdovsky

DAVID R. GODINE · PUBLISHER · BOSTON

First published in 1990 by
David R. Godine Publisher, Inc.
Horticultural Hall
300 Massachusetts Avenue
Boston, Massachusetts 02115

The following poems appeared in *Laughing Time: Collected Non-
sense* by William Jay Smith, published by Farrar, Straus &
Giroux, 1990, copyright © 1953, 1955, 1957, 1990 by William
Jay Smith: "Cat," "Dog," "Cow," "Zebra," "Tiger," "Owl,"
"Ostrich," "Unicorn," "Butterfly," and "Penguin." The quat-
rain "Squirrel" is the opening stanza of "Autumn," which ap-
peared in *Collected Poems: 1939-1989* by William Jay Smith,
published by Charles Scribner's Sons, 1990, copyright © 1957,
1990 by William Jay Smith. All the other poems appear here for
the first time.

Library of Congress Catalog Card Number: 90-55276
ISBN: 0-87923-865-8

First Edition
Printed in the United States of America

To
Marissa and Alexandre

CONTENTS

Cat
Dog
Rooster
Tiger
Zebra
Cow
Lady Bug
Tortoise
Owl
Ostrich
Unicorn
Butterfly
Flamingo
Penguin
Prairie Chicken

Sheep
Llama
Duck
Vulture
Porcupine
Kiwi
Lamb
Squirrel
Sage Grouse
Turkey
Goose
Bald Eagle
Water Buffalo
Peacock

Cat

Cats are not at all like people,
　　Cats are Cats.

People wear stockings and sweaters,
Overcoats, mufflers, and hats.
Cats wear nothing: they lie by the fire
For twenty-four hours if they desire.
They do NOT rush out to the office,
They do NOT have interminable chats,
They do NOT play Old Maid and Checkers,
They do NOT wear bright yellow spats.

People, of course, will always be people,
　　But Cats are Cats.

Dog

Dogs are quite a bit like people,
    Or so it seems to me somehow.
Like people, Dogs go anywhere,
They swim in the sea, they leap through the air,
They bark and growl, they sit and stare,
They even wear what people wear.
Look at that Poodle with a hat on its noodle,
Look at that Boxer in a long silver-fox fur,
Look at that Whippet in its calico tippet,
Look at that Sealyham in diamonds from Rotterdam,
Look at that Afghan wrapped in an afghan,
Look at that Chow down there on a dhow
All decked out for some big powwow
With Pekinese waiting to come kowtow.
    Don't they all look just like people?
    People you've *seen* somewhere? Bowwow!

Rooster

When the stars above begin to fade
And morning streaks across the sky,
A bugler in bright uniform—
Red interwoven with gold braid,
Panache of flashing plumes unswirled—
Steps proudly out against the blue,
And with his "Cock-a-doodle-doo,"
Salutes the day, wakes up the world.

Tiger

A hunter cried out when he spotted a Tiger,
"What a beautiful rug that creature would make!"
The Tiger growled: he did not agree;
He chased the hunter up a tree.
The hunter's gun went Bang! Bang! Bang!
Zing! Zing! Zing! the bullets sang;
A bunch of bananas plopped to the ground.
The Tiger laughed as he danced around.
He laughed so very hard, poor fellow,
Off flew his stripes of black and yellow.

When lightning flashes through the sky
And the candle glows in my cat's eye;
When thunder rolls from organ pipes,
I think I see those Tiger stripes,
I think I see them whizzing by
In streaks of lightning through the sky.

Zebra

Are Zebras black with broad white stripes,
Or are they really white with black?
Answer me that and I'll give you some candy
And a green-and-yellow jumping jack.

Cow

Cows are not supposed to fly,
And so, if you should see
A spotted Cow go flying by
Above a pawpaw tree
In a porkpie hat with a green umbrella,
Then run right down the road and tell a
Lady selling sarsaparilla,
Lemon soda and vanilla,
So she can come here and tell me!

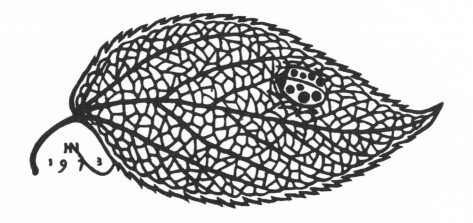

Lady Bug

Lady Bug, Lady Bug,
Life is so brief,
Why linger so long
On that lacy leaf?

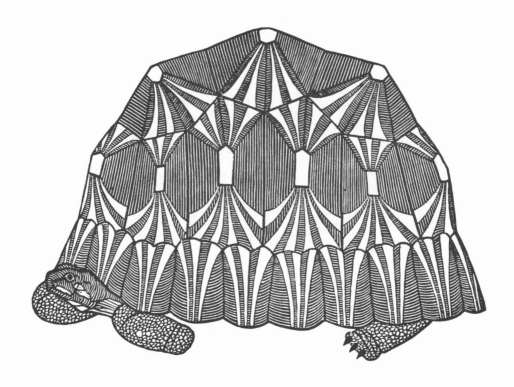

Tortoise

The Tortoise, when it makes its rounds,
Does not proceed by leaps and bounds.
It takes its time. It eats and sleeps,
And then sets out, and on it creeps.
Then stops again. And eats and sleeps.
Sets out again. And on it creeps.

Owl

The Owl that lives in the old oak tree
Opens his eyes and cannot see
When it's clear as day to you and me;
But not long after the sun goes down
And the Church Clock strikes in Tarrytown
And Nora puts on her green nightgown,
He opens his big bespectacled eyes
And shuffles out of the hollow tree,
And flies and flies
                and flies and flies,
And flies and flies
                and flies and flies.

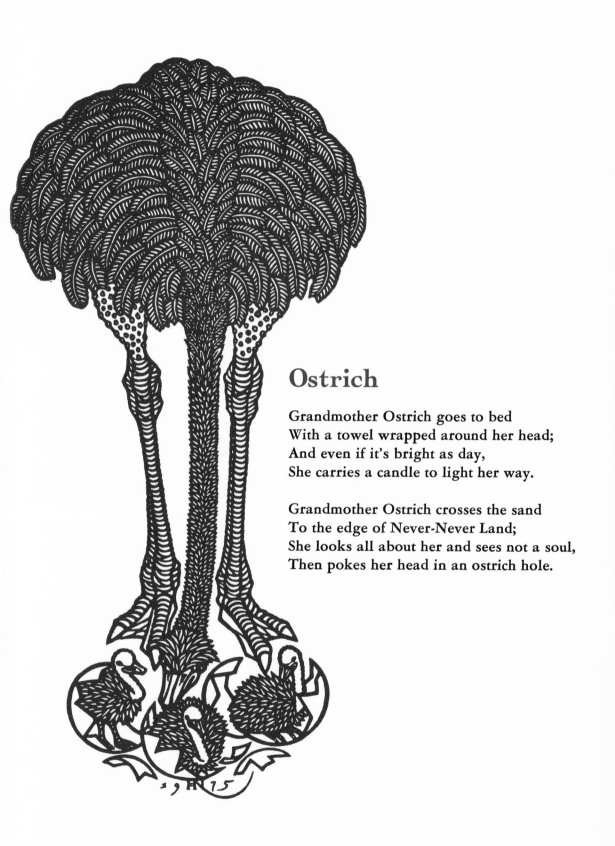

Ostrich

Grandmother Ostrich goes to bed
With a towel wrapped around her head;
And even if it's bright as day,
She carries a candle to light her way.

Grandmother Ostrich crosses the sand
To the edge of Never-Never Land;
She looks all about her and sees not a soul,
Then pokes her head in an ostrich hole.

Unicorn

The Unicorn with the long white horn
    Is beautiful and wild.
He gallops across the forest green
So quickly that he's seldom seen
Where Peacocks their blue feathers preen
    And strawberries grow wild.
He flees the hunter and the hounds,
Upon black earth his white hoof pounds,
Over cold mountain streams he bounds
    And comes to a meadow mild;
There, when he kneels to take his nap,
He lays his head in a lady's lap
    As gently as a child.

Butterfly

Of living creatures most I prize
Black-spotted yellow Butterflies
Sailing softly through the skies,

Whisking light from each sunbeam,
Gliding over field and stream—
Like fans unfolding in a dream,

Like fans of gold lace flickering
Before a drowsy elfin king
For whom the thrush and linnet sing—

Soft and beautiful and bright
As hands that move to touch the light
When Mother leans to say good night.

Flamingo

When it stands on one leg,
Head under one wing,
Far away
From everything,
It seems to say
In its shocking pink:
"I do as I please,
Whatever you think;
I do as I please,
Whatever you think."

Penguin

I think it must be very nice
To stroll about upon the ice,
Night and day, day and night,
Wearing only black and white,
Always in your Sunday best—
Black tailcoat and pearl-white vest.
To stroll about so pleasantly
Beside the cold and silent sea
Would really suit me to a T!
I think it must be very nice
To stroll with Penguins on the ice.

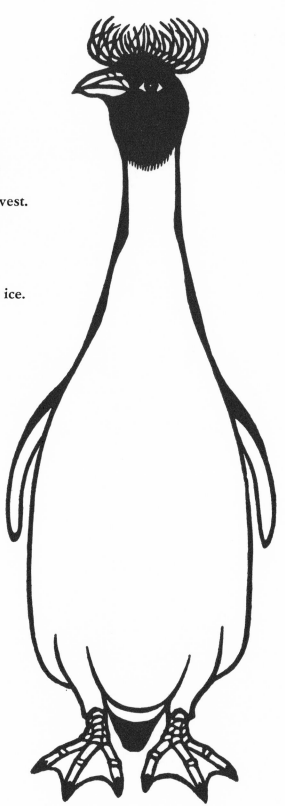

Prairie Chicken

Look at him there in that prairie dirt:
Did any bird ever look so dapper,
All laced up in that ruffled shirt,
With a high stiff collar, all prim and proper?

He prances around for a very long while;
His heart beats faster, his footsteps quicken:
He looks for someone who likes his style,
He looks for another Prairie Chicken.

Sheep

Blank face staring out
From a gray woollen heap—
Goes over the fence
When I go to sleep.

Llama

I learned about the Llama when I learned to spell;
But is it because the beast is so long
That its name is written with a double *l*?

Duck

On the farmyard pond it paddles around
With its broad flat bill and its wide webbed feet;
And calls Quack-Quack to its friends on the ground
And darts its head under for something to eat.

Vulture

The Vulture has a thin and scrawny neck
And scraggly feathers like broken chains;
It circles above you when you eat,
Then swoops to remove whatever remains.

Porcupine

A fat pincushion
All covered with pins,
Where his middle leaves off
And his bottom begins.

Kiwi

When other birds go flying by,
The Kiwi gazes at the ground.
A bird that walks and cannot fly
Has little interest in the sky;
It simply gazes at the ground,
And walks and walks and walks around
And walks and walks and walks around.

Lamb

When he frolics about,
All lightness and laughter,
There's no darkness, no doubt,
But joy ever after.

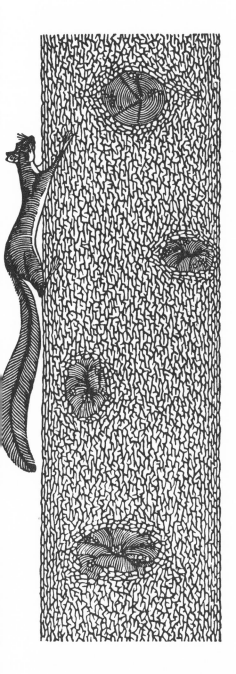

Squirrel

The color of stone when leaves are yellow,
Comes the Squirrel, a capital C,
With tail atilt like a violincello,
Comes the Squirrel musically.

Sage Grouse

When he starts to rant
And swell up like a plant,
Better let the Grouse
Out of the house.

Turkey

With his fantail spread as if for a show,
The Turkey gobbler gobbles and struts.
He's a beautiful bird, he wants you to know—
No *if*'s, no *and*'s, no *but*'s.

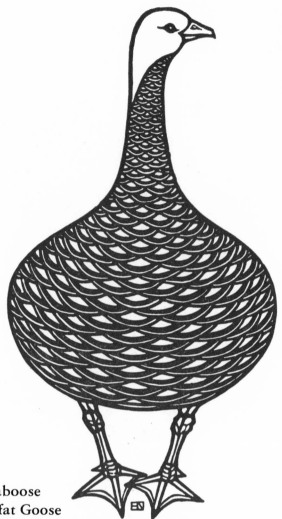

Goose

On a crazy caboose
Rides a silly fat Goose
    To a land Marco Polo never explored,
Where in grass long and wavy
You eat giblet gravy
    And the money you spend is the money you hoard;
Where the money you earn
Is money to burn,
    And nobody works and nobody's bored;
Where uphill the river
Flows on forever,
    And time that is lost is quickly restored.

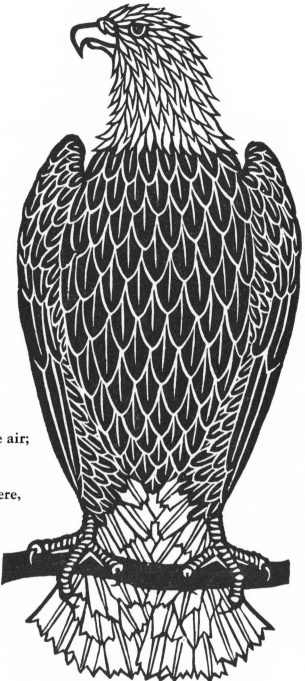

Bald Eagle

The Eagle rules with majesty
The cloud-capped kingdom of the air;
And yet his royal flight's so free
That he becomes for you and me,
When we look up and see him there,
The emblem of our liberty.

Water Buffalo

The finest animal I know
Is the good black Water Buffalo.
    When the sun of the East beats down on the clay
    And coconuts fall and palm trees sway,
    He plods through the rice field day after day.
With graceful long horns, he is gentle and slow:
    I love the Water Buffalo!

Peacock

When the Peacock proudly ambles by,
He has, in his blue-green tail unfurled,
More dazzling spots than stars in the sky
Or capitals on a map of the world.

Birds and Beasts has been designed and printed letterpress from Monotype by W. Thomas Taylor of Austin, Texas. The text face is Garamond Bold, a face that has its origins in the designs of the French Renaissance and was part of the series of "historic revivals" initiated by the Monotype Corporation of London during the 1920s. Actually, the types we now call "Garamond" were based on excellent copies cut by Jean Jannon in the seventeenth century. Nonetheless, the type remains a singularly beautiful example of the crisp, brisk designs so favored in Paris and Lyons during that time as French typographers moved away from the northern Gothic types and toward the lighter Italian models.

The display face for the titles and heads is Cochin, a face based on copperplate engravings of eighteenth-century France and adopted for the Monotype in 1917 by Sol Hess. The italic is especially graceful, a lucid interpretation of handwriting and formal engraving. The book was printed on Mohawk Superfine, an entirely acid-free sheet.

An edition of 6,000 copies has been printed, of which 1,000 copies, specially bound and signed by the author, have been reserved for the members of

HOC VOLO

This is copy number:

ABOUT THE AUTHOR

William Jay Smith was born in 1918 in Winnfield, Louisiana, and studied at Washington University, Columbia, and Oxford (as a Rhodes Scholar). He was Poetry Consultant to the Library of Congress 1968-1970, and has been a member of the Academy and Institute of Arts and Letters since 1975. In 1990 he published *Collected Poems 1939-1989* and *Laughing Time: Selected Nonsense*. Jacques Hnizdovsky did four woodcuts for Smith's *The Traveler's Tree: Selected Poems* (1980) and illustrated Smith's anthology *A Green Place: Modern Poems* (1982). They had worked for some time on *Birds and Beasts* before Hnizdovsky's death.

ABOUT THE ARTIST

Jacques Hnizdovsky was a woodcutter and artist who emigrated from Bohemia to America. His first book, *Flora Exotica*, was published by Godine in 1972 and contained fifteen woodcuts printed in color with a text by Gordon DeWolfe. Throughout his life, which ended in 1985, Hnizdovsky remained a master craftsman in the European tradition, an artist whose interpretations of animals, plants, and figures were immediately recognizable for their vigor, strength, and quiet humor. This book, printed from line cuts made from his proofs, is a testament to his particular vision and personal genius.